How to Tell Your Children About the Holocaust

Ruth Mandel

McGilligan Books

National Library of Canada Cataloguing in Publication

Mandel, Ruth
     How to tell your children about the Holocaust / Ruth Mandel.
ISBN 1-894692-06-3
     1. Holocaust, Jewish (1939-1945)—Poetry. I. Title.

PS8576.A54111H68 2003   C811'.6   C2003-904052-6

Poems from this collection have been published on various websites, including *Women and the Holocaust*, and included in the anthologies *Vintage 97/98*, *She's Gonna Be* and *Never Again, A History of the Holocaust* and published in the journals and newsletters *Parchment: A Journal of Jewish Writing, The Fiddlehead, Prairie Fire, Canadian Woman Studies, Antigonish Review, Outlook Magazine, Fireweed, Taddle Creek, Kavananah Newsletter, The Hidden Child Foundation Newsletter, If Not Now, Jewish Women's Forum, Contemporary Verse 2, Swedish Women's Education Association Newsletter, The Holocaust Remembrance Committee of Toronto Newsletter.*

Editor: Jannie Edwards
Copy editor: Noreen Shanahan
Cover design: Carl Mandel
Layout: Heather Guylar
Colour Photographs: Ian Clifford, pages 10, 52, 72, 79, 82, 87, 94, 161 upper;
Judith Mandel, pages 64, 118, 159, 161 lower.
Black and white photographs: Photographers unknown
Cover photograph: Photographer unknown, *Henryk and Roman Mandel, Cracow, 1939*
Stitching: Rachel MacHenry
Handwritten fonts: Ray Mandel

With thanks to Ian Clifford for scanning, preparing and making the photographs and the cover art possible.

McGilligan Books gratefully acknowledges the support of The Canada Council for the Arts, the Ontario Arts Council and the Ontario Book Publisher Tax Credit for our publishing program and Proplan Limited for supporting this book.
Printed in Canada

Canada Council   Conseil des Arts
for the Arts   du Canada

CONTENTS

TRAVELLING

WHO SPEAKS

INTRODUCTION

Ruth Mandel has approached the difficult and important problem of *How to Tell Your Children About the Holocaust* through poetry. It is an impressive endeavour. Before writing more about her book, I must, as parliamentarians say, "declare an interest". Sixty years ago it was my good fortune to have been brought up, between the ages of three and seven, with Ruth Mandel's mother, who was even younger than I was. My status was that of wartime evacuee from Britain: her parents took me in for four years.

When Ruth was born, it gave me particular pleasure. Her mother had married a Holocaust survivor, Ray Mandel, and unknown to any of us then, Ruth was to become the articulate voice of the "second generation", as they are known – the children of survivors. I was so struck by one of her poems that I included it in my book for young people, *Never Again, A History of the Holocaust.*

Ruth Mandel's poems seem to me to have particular resonance not only for survivors, and for the children of survivors, but also for those who, like myself, have no personal Holocaust experience or survivor parents or grandparents. We too will be able to put ourselves in her place on that Friday night just over ten years ago, when she asked her father what had happened to him during the Holocaust, and he would not tell her; and when, on returning to her own home that Friday night, she found an answering machine message from her mother telling her: "stay away from your father" (poem: "Round 1 Goes to the Parents").

Every poem catches the imagination with its varied, powerful imagery. Each one can be read and absorbed on its own, or as part of the evolving whole. Some make an impact long after they have been read. Step-Grandmother Nika crying "at every Passover seder" will live with the reader at his or her seder nights (poem: "Learning"). The nine lines about her father in hiding, ending "No heart beats allowed", is stark in its simplicity and power (poem: "Occupied Cracow").

Every poem not only conveys dramatic, somber, strongly visual or emotional moments, but makes clear, in its particular imagery, the vastness and incomprehensibility of the Holocaust as "smell, sound, sight, a scream without end, ringing, and ringing, and ringing" (poem: "The Holocaust Is"). Ruth Mandel presents us with many undead demons, not least in her line, which is both a question and a statement, "How far the continuing reach" (poem: "Questionnaire — Grandchildren and Great-Grandchildren of Survivors").

People of all ages will find this book both enlightening and disturbing. It is as much addressed to the adults who feel that they must tell their children about the Holocaust as to those children themselves; and the "children" of her title can be of all ages, just as, at the start of the twenty-first century, the children of the survivors — like Ruth Mandel herself — are mature adults, many of them, like her, with children of their own.

These poems will be read, and re-read, with deep emotion, by men and women of goodwill of many different backgrounds and generations — and read by parents to their children.

Sir Martin Gilbert
April 2003

For Elzbieta and Ziva and Tai'o and

Apartment 9, 4 Rakovicka Street, Cracow, 1996

Divining

DIVINING

Through osmosis I recall :
the homes of frightened saviours
the apartment door knocks
you flee through the kitchen
into a small closet
space enough
behind the springs of an old mattress
to entrust your hiding life
all eyes on the door knob

your crystal ball

ROUND 1 GOES TO THE PARENTS

Shabbat dinner at my parents house,
Friday March 12 1990, I asked
pointblank,
"Dad, what happened to you in the holocaust?"

No answer.
"I'm twenty-six. I need to know. If you can't tell me
yourself, lend me the video of your interview
at the Holocaust Documentation Centre, instead."

"No Way." Dad said, flat out, glaring.
"Okay, if you won't let me see your tape, I can
view it at the Centre, where it is available by your
consent, to the general public."

The air tightened. I knew
I had made a mistake.
Stricken, Mom watched me.
Watched me hurl us

into a ferocious galaxy, blast into
her life's work, the invisible
constellations of protection she held in orbit
around each of us.

Lines drawn.
I left in a huff,

determined to fight my dad
for his life, our past.

At my home, my mother ambushed me
from my answering machine.

"Ruth you stay away from your father.
You don't know what you're doing. You
don't know what you're getting into. He
doesn't want to talk about it. Don't push.
Just leave him alone. You will destroy him."

Pointblank.
How to ask?
How to tell?

LEARNING

I.

Not To Laugh

My step-grandmother Nika cried at every Passover seder.
Her tears, unacknowledged commands.
We avoided her eyes.

One of us might laugh, toss a head back,
off guard. An accidental glance might slip her way.
Snap! Eyes caught.
Caught in the act of forgetting. Caught
in the act of living. Caught
not mourning, for one split second.

Those sore eyes. Chastising eyes.
We paid the price soon enough - learning
not to look.

Not to laugh.

II.

The Set Up

It's a set up :
Everything is laid out
to offer you everything

and then hate you for taking it.
To give you choices
and always let you know
you have made

the wrong one:

They died and we struggled to make a life for you, that you should be happy, and look at you, smiling - Shame on you.

We worked hard so you wouldn't have to, but you, what do you do, you're not a doctor - What have you made of yourself?

We saved money all our life, so you should be secure, and there you go, a home, a car - What do you know from pain?

We did everything for you so you would have all you want, and look at you, living your own life - This is thanks?

They all died, the whole family lost, life goes on, you should have a family, but marry a goy? keep two dogs? You think this is funny?

You shouldn't suffer like we did. So many Jews died in misery. For what? You must be happy, make up our loss, it must never happen again, never be forgotten, it must live within you, you are rebirth, joy, life itself ... And, tst, look at you carrying on, sassing, joking, laughing aloud, weeping at your own sadness - How could you?

III.

How Could You?

Of course,
the set up is decipherable only
to you. No words
you can put your finger on
or scream back.
To others, you are always
reading too much into things.

The bristly language of eyebrow muscles,
corners of mouths,
crests of shoulders,
posture of the hands,
breath on its way in, or worse

on its way out.

OCCUPIED CRACOW

He was a small child
my father,
in 1942,
seven years old.

Hiding, still.
Motionless for two years.
Two
Years

No heart beats allowed.

HEART : NIKA, MY STEP-GRANDMOTHER SPEAKS

You can ask questions about your dad's family, but your dad's family I didn't, I didn't know his mother I didn't know his brother. I knew everything about them, what happened to them, it's terrible.   I don't remember much

After the war, 1945, we went for the help to the Jewish Committee in Cracow, you know? Everybody was looking for somebody, you understand, who is alive, who survived, help. I didn't have nothing. And there he was, Mechel, with your father Ray, such a little boy, and I came with my sister Sala. As soon as Mechel saw me, he said, *This is the one that I will marry*. And he didn't let me go. I, you think I wanted to marry? I didn't want to marry yet, I didn't care.   I was broken in pieces

Fifty years over, and my memory, no, some people remember everything, every moment, every, they remember. Listen Ruthie, you have the tea, yah, take a cookie, it's very good cookies, oatmeal. I loved, I fell in love with little Ray. He was such a darling! Mechel, we got married, 19maybe45 or something, I think, I don't know what day, I really don't remember.   We were so run down, we don't know nothing what was happening

I was married in my home. I was living with my sister Sala, Mechel was living there too, I don't remember. I would tell you, but I am thinking, I am thinking if he was there too. This was his apartment.   We went there to live because we didn't have where to go

My sister Fritka lived with Max somewhere else. Fritka and Max were married before, they had a little boy and he got killed. They killed him, Polaks. She kept him, till eight months and later he start to talk a little bit and she gave him away to Polaks that they know, and another little girl from Cracow, Silinger, and the Polaks came and killed them. The same the whole my family they killed, the Polaks.   The Germans didn't know like that who is a Jew

Ray's mother Henia had died, maybe January, maybe February. I don't remember how. She must to die in the hospital. I don't know. I think she die when she was having the baby, I hear, I think so. I think a girl. I don't know who told me. Maybe Mechel told me. I swear to God I don't remember. Somebody told me this. I don't know why we never talk about.   Your father doesn't know?

I don't know why we never talk about, by God, what is, why not, do I have something to hide or what? There's nothing to hide. You know how many people were married? But what was to hide here, you know what happened in the war time. You know there was a couples, plenty. They had a child, and the husband killed the baby. Yah, a lot of this was happening. They wanted to live and that baby wouldn't, would be impossible. They were just married and they went and killed the babies. No, this was right?   The will to life is so terrible then you have to kill a baby, the baby didn't know nothing, it was just born

It was after the war when Henia had the baby. But everything was arranged, the hospital, and the people, and the nurses, and the doctor, everything, but I don't know. She must be, I think, if you are sick for, if you have here in the back, how you call this, then you can't have your baby. Help me, you know when you, it's a sickness, here, here I think, when you don't cure, it develops. From the war, sure, she got this sickness from the war.   I wish, I wish she would be alive

She was a very very fine woman. Mechel talked about her. He was carrying her picture, with the three of you grandchildren, here, all his life after the war.

Here, right on his heart

Henia Mandel (born Schindla), photograph used for wartime identification papers, 1942

Current name Name given at birth Name(s) used during
the war Date of birth Place of origin Place of residence
before the war How large was your family before the
war Were you married Did you have children Where
were you when the war reached you Describe your
war-time experiences in detail Did you have a business
that was confiscated Were you forced to stop your
profession How did you survive the war Were you
forced to split up your family Did you pay someone to
hide your children Were you able to visit them Were
you hidden by someone you knew or by a stranger Did
you escape from a round up Was your family taken
from you at a concentration camp Did you pass as a
non-Jew with partisans Did you use several false
identities How did you fight back Were you ever
tortured Did your actions ever bring punishment on
others What do you think kept you alive Did you
connect with others or struggle alone Was there
someone you took care of Was there a thought or belief
that kept you going Was it nothing but chance During
the war did you hear about family members or friends
who were murdered or died How did you know the
war was over When and where were you liberated By
whom What did you do after the war Were you able to
return home Did you attempt to retrieve your children
Had any of them been murdered How many family
members survived the war Were you able to reunite
Had non-Jews taken over your home Were your

possessions returned Were you threatened or chased away Did they harm or kill any of your surviving family or friends Were you able to resettle and work Did you find out what happened to each family member Are you still searching for records of survival or death Are you still searching for a family member who may be alive Do you catch yourself staring at any face with fleeting familiarity Current place of residence Have you seen neo-Nazi graffiti or violence in your neighbourhood How does it affect you Current occupation Current health Current marital status Is your spouse a holocaust survivor Did you have children after the war Do your children born after the war know about your children who were murdered List some of the ways your holocaust experience has affected your life What do you tell people about your holocaust experience How do they respond Are there experiences you will never tell   ?

POSTCARD TO THE HOLOCAUST

dear grandmother henia,

     sometimes, when we sat around the dinner table,
I would notice zaidi mechel's eyes locked on me

     when we compare my face with your old photographs,
we say   *My, it is incredible how much Ruth looks like her!*
but we wouldn't be so amazed, if you were still alive, if we
could remember you, if you hadn't been murdered.   yearning
black and white photographs leak a tiny speck of your blood
through their thinning silver emulsion   onto my face

DAYBREAK

Delicate side table braces
hot tea   ominous tissues   colourful hard
candies   promissory business cards within
arm's reach. "Your father
is a holocaust survivor?
My parents are too," she offers.
"Do you think that has affected
your life?"

"Definitely."

We each lean back   nodding agreement
a ticking box now set between us   my counsellor opens
"Would you like to talk about that?"
I shrug "Sure,
I guess I could."

Forged identification document using non-Jewish names: Mechel, Henia,
Roman Mandel as Jan, Helena (wife), Stanislaw (son) Lorek, 1943

ALL WE HAVE

Photographs -
they're all we have.
Or, all we think we have

                  like God.

We strive to earn our way into their hearts:
whisper, adore, worship, clamour.
They ignore, elude. Trapped,
they offer all
and give nothing.
We hold them,
they hold us. Rather, they *could*
but won't.

Suggestive appearances
bewilder
> *There they are, exactly as they were.*
> *Some were younger than we are now, and some*
> *would by now be dead.*

Force us to realize
what is gone is gone,
and long ago.
> *See how he looks like me, he has my nose, my wide mouth,*
> *the dip of the hairline into the forehead.*

Family semblances mollify
and incite.

We aim our panting souls through two dimensions
to theirs, hope they will find our breath,
would give up our lungs in a flash.
Our family of paper, they pat
the cushion beside them, invite us to settle, hint
they will reveal themselves soon. Never
turn their heads.

The rare snapshots.
Caught head-on, mid-stride.
We implore them
resume movement, keep striding
toward us,
toward embrace.

Photographs. We must handle carefully
what few we have - a clutch
of feeding doves, they may
fly off.

Mesmerized, we look and look, endow them
with past and future. As if they might
reveal ours.

Portraits promise the most.
In studios, our families posed
their still, mute stories. Hardened and faultless
they meet us face to face,
but not eye to eye.
We grip the brittle line
of their gaze, battle the immutable hold
of the X marked on the wall

just over the photographer's shoulder,
just over ours.
We beg donned faces to soften, beg
the stiff, obdurate yellow-brown papers to turn
inside out. Show us
    Which of those props are real?
    Is that a dress she usually wore?
    How much of that really is us?

Looking and looking,
doesn't mean there is anything
we can see.

            Like God.

Nazi-issued documents torment us.
Photographed
by force.
A lone, fearful face
held captive
by the official stamp. The iron eagle glares,
square head and hooked beak turn sharp right,
fierce talons circle the swastika, wings
mighty and wide
crush the face
against the page.

Authenticated by patchy purple ink,
fingered by officers, police, guards.
Touched
by us.

Wanting to rescue
from the savage bird
we scratch too hard
the old, dry surface, and
regret the damage we have done,
scramble to repair wounds

we did not inflict.
Pleading.
Them. Us.

Seal in archival envelopes,
sturdy albums,
vigilant glass frames.

Dear Photographs, we choke,

> *call them back*
> *call them back into being*

Our family of paper -
All we have.

Defy time,
enforce permanence,
keep watch.

God is going to be here soon

God will never come

HENIA : MEMORIES OF MY GRANDMOTHER

(i)

I remember   my grandmother Henia I am told
I resemble my father's mother I have never met
never known never touched
who smells of dust one of the few
who is buried has a gravestone my grandmother
who sounds like the cry of a baby and a mother
dying together in childbirth because she was so sick
hiding for two years a closet in Cracow dying in childbirth
the end of the war

she feels like open arms because some day I will go
to Poland visit her grave and plant flowers that will smell
like an embrace in her Friday kitchen taste
like the words we never bind
like the feelings we cannot flowers
that will carry the silence
her son my father has kept
the silence our visit will cherish
and break

returning us more
than intact

(ii)

I imagine   walking alone into a cemetery in Cracow alone
because my husband is elsewhere
his absence a decision we have made
I know where to go recall
the description my cousin gave to find my grandmother's grave
I do not have the work nor the peace
of a search
as I approach the grave that weighted feeling my legs
drop away in heaviness from the part of me that realizes
just where I am
just what I am doing
just how hard this is

as I approach the grave that hurried feeling my legs
move quicker to the place my breath anticipates my knees
against her grass my hands against her stone
my eyes upon the inscription
buckling
the dark marble is inscribed for Henia and
above it a plaque inscribed for my uncle Henryk
her son my father's brother
murdered three years before her

my eyes upon the inscriptions my arms thrown wide
I am present for the dead who have always for better or worse
been present for me

TATTOO

On my way into the concert
the usher stamps
a blue star
on my arm.

I can come
and go

as I please

dear great aunt erna,

Anyone who knows you would believe it easily, even expect it. They have had to strap worn, grey canvas around your wrists and across your legs. To keep you there, prevent you from kicking your feet over the edge, wresting yourself out of the bed, wrenching those I.V.s out of your arm, the oxygen tube out of your throat and walking right out of the hospital, probably unaware that your lungs cannot breathe, your legs cannot carry you. Your mind, having a mind of its own, would just walk on out, regardless.

Memory is a kind of oxygen.

The survivor in you ready to take care of yourself, by your own means. But, if you flail and kick yourself free as you are trying, we would lose you, on foot, to an unwalkable, vague and dreaded landscape. They have bound you, to protect you from your desire to flee. One strap wraps itself just under the tattoo Auschwitz gave you. Clever Auschwitz, keeping itself alive, on your arm.

Memory is a kind of ruin.

The tube in your throat makes it impossible for you to speak, your eyes, bore through us and plead. Occasionally, you write a word on a blank white page, pencil shaking in restrained fingers, barely pressing against the page, illegible marks which we try gravely to make out. And your strapped hands, they too, gesture and implore. All your signals scream, *"OUT."*

A kind of terror.

Your first baby, Bina Rachel, born in Tarnopol Ghetto in 1940. And died there, exactly one year later, on Yom Kippur. "A natural death." Language tortures us. *Natural?* Relative to the other deaths. Meaning she died in your helpless, hungry arms. And was not shot, not smothered, not thrown to life or to death, from a racing gas-bound train. A dead bundle, swaddled in your ribbon-thin hands.

A kind of burial.

And later, your husband smuggled you and his sister out of the ghetto. False papers named you, *Marysia Loska*, the last time you saw him. You and she were arrested, because she *looked Jewish*, and only you had your papers. In jail, the guards questioned. You lied, and pointed to your blue eyes, all those fools needed to be convinced you fit their smug aryan definitions.

Memory is a kind of proof.

Convincing them of a false address in a non-Jewish part of town was dangerous. When they investigated and countered that you had given a street address higher than the numbers actually went, you insisted they had heard incorrectly, persuading them you had said *8* and not *18*. Persuading them that your neighbours denied knowing you because you had committed some disgracing, unmentionable deed. You spun stories deftly, never sure if they would save your life.

A kind of unravelling.

Unknown to you, your sister-in-law was already murdered. You tried to escape from jail and were sent to Auschwitz, where your expert sewing saved your life. And to Birkenau, where you continued to sew, perhaps uniforms for the guards, vestments for the officers, dresses for their wives - you never said. Three years of saving your life every moment. You, a Jew, hiding in a death camp, as a Pole who was caught with a Jew. Emerging to a depleted world, to learn of your husband's death. A death which even now you cannot bear to speak.

A kind of wail.

Years later in Toronto, you hosted every Passover seder in your apartment. Your brother, my Zaidi Mechel, took us through the archaic Hagadah until his death. When I wrote a new one for our family, you enjoyed the chance to read aloud and tell us of Passovers in your childhood. The foods you prepared were something tangible to take us back and usher us forward. You have been our lived memory, our certain memory. Our living memory. You have remembered for us, generously, openly, without demands upon us. A model, teaching us to remember faithfully, yet still enjoy life's other colours. What questions I could bear to ask, bear to inflict, you answered with affection, with details, impressions, dailiness, events.

A kind of love.

Remembering was substantive and specific. We sat with my tape recorder running. You introduced me to your sister in law Henia, my father's mother - as you knew her - your girlish awe and envy, her urbaneness, intelligence, sophistication. *Elegance*, your word exactly, "Oh, how I looked up to her, me a young girl from the country, she was married and living in the city, I could just sit and watch, everything beautiful, the way she walked, dressed, how she talked to me."

Memory is a kind of family.

And you introduced me to your nephew, my father, as a child. Your head tilted fondly and your glinting eyes gazing off to the side, animated, as though about to join a giddy family table in the corner of the room. Your attention fixed there, you chuckled and described him, circling the crowded table to nibble food off people's plates - or am I confusing this with how you remember me as a child.

A kind of fusion.

You helped me draw the family tree from which I grew, create remembrances where I had none. You helped people the sets, props and wardrobe on a distant, smashed stage. Told me who entered, exited, crossed, returned or was never seen again. The kinds of details that make my eyes flood and my sinuses rush in anguish. Make me realize fiercely what we have lost. What is missing. Why we are lonely.

A kind of script.

And even then, not getting a photo of you, of your arm. And even then, not covering it all. And even then I tired, not making as much effort as I should have, not staying longer. Knowing that I was leaving, and you were staying in your apartment to contend with the cast of loved ones my questions had invited into your home - some still struggling to live, some in the throes of horrendous deaths, some waiting, some watching - all of them our blood, all of them flowing.

A kind of danger.

Your daughter Sharon said you recently pointed to my wedding invitation, still posted in the kitchen of your home and said, "I was in Sweden." My husband's Swedish background has always been a source of cherished memory for you - the place of your liberation, your first smorgasbord, the hotel sheltering Displaced Persons, overlooking the sea, safe haven at the end of the war. *The end of the war* - Sweden made those words possible for you. Working again as a seamstress, this time for kind women and for pay. A time of recuperation before returning to assess absolute loss. Wicked and unmovable loss.

Memory is a kind of stone.

And now, your body is emaciated, again. Disoriented and distressed, you have forgotten how to eat and do not want to remember. Or cannot. Your hand knocks Sharon's spoon away. A stroke brought you to the hospital, where you forgot how to breathe and do not want to remember. Or cannot. The ventilator tricks your body into remaining alive. Some days your eyes open, others they do not. You take my offered hand, squeeze my palm and weave your fingers in and out of mine.

A kind of loom.

On Fridays, Sharon lights the hospital-approved electric candles for you. For you and for God. God, whom you have talked to each and every Shabbat, at sunset, eyes closed gently. You lit the candles, sheltered them with your hands and whispered once the blessing through your fingers. Your arms circled slowly to shepherd their light, spread it among us and across time. Head bowed and eyes covered by your fingers, once more the blessing, this time your throat still and just your lips reciting. You, the women before you, beside you, after you, with you.

Memory is a kind of prayer.

A kind of oxygen   a ruin   a terror   Memory is a kind of burial a proof   an unravelling   a wail   Memory is a kind of love   a family a fusion   a script   Memory is a kind of danger   a stone   a loom. A prayer.

At seventy-six your memory is walking briskly away from you, leaving you,   and leaving us,   behind.

Who will do the remembering now? Who is remembering now.

Eulogy, Erna Weintraub — March 15, 1918 - March 10, 1995

Erna Mandel, later Weintraub, Cracow, 1946

ACCORDING TO MY DAD

Death is waiting.
Death is waiting for you to drop your guard.
Death will tear your guard to shreds
and not wait.

Death wants you.
Death wants you to suddenly want life.
That is death's favourite moment
and death is listening carefully for that inaudible shift.

Death is the only certainty.
Beware of the impulse to survive.
It will get your hopes up,
possibly even save you.

Death will not surprise you.
It will be exactly what you have feared all along.

According to my dad.

MUSEUM OF US

A child is like a butterfly, they say,
they say a butterfly is free.

You were a child then,
Father. When the rules began
to descend like nets
your wings were bound
by the yellow star.
When the decrees were aimed like pins
your parents hid you
in someone else's home.
That small closet   a jar
tight around you.
The caution and the fear   a lid.

When you play and tease, Father,
I wonder about your brightness and flight
before.
And when you are brittled by nights
that rack you
into memory's glass case,
I know

the Shoah
is the bottle in which
we are held.

POSTCARD TO THE HOLOCAUST

dear great uncle salig,

As you speak, I listen, bear witness to you, to you remembering your past. How you could not make any sense of why you survived the war, how being singled out for life felt like a judgment against you, as you learned every blood relative you had ever known had been murdered. You are specific. Forty-four. Forty-four grandparents, adults and children.

Your long, laboured, incremental counting. Drawn out over days and months and years. Pieced from witnesses, talk, hearsay, whispers, cusses, insinuation, uncovered secrets, Nazi records. No physical remains. Not a single burial, not one grave. Endless hopelessness, endless hope.

You gaze at me and through me and away from me, rock your head from side to side in fresh pain and disbelief. No one to reunite with, to bring comfort, forgive you, set off with. You tell me you fled your home town, not prepared to drop your guard just because it was the end of the war. Eventually found your way to a Displaced Persons camp in Germany, where you met Erna and married. You went together to Cracow, where Erna had a nephew and a brother. My dad, Zaidi Mechel, and his new wife Nika.

To immigrate to Canada, passports were required. You wrote to the priest in your village, asked him to find any records. Any. Nazis had destroyed almost all evidence of Jewish life. The priest was able to find only one record of birth, that of your brother, Jacob.

And this is the name you have been known by, officially,
ever since. Jacob Weintraub. The name on your passport, prescription
bottles, legal documents, the name you sign over and over. Not
Salig, your name, the name we call you, but your brother's.

You quiet briefly, and then remark that you recently heard
of two brothers reuniting at a Florida restaurant, after fifty years.

Eulogy, Salig Weintraub — November 25, 1911 - August 28, 1998

QUESTIONNAIRE
SPOUSES OF HOLOCAUST SURVIVORS

Name Name given at birth Date of birth Place of origin Current marital status Age during war years Did your family do anything to help Jews in Europe during the war How did you feel when the extent of the genocide was revealed Did your parents try to protect you from knowing How did you meet your spouse How much did you know about the holocaust before you met Did you know your fiancé/e was a holocaust survivor when you married How did you come to know what had happened to your spouse Were you the first person she ever told Was it painful for him to speak of For you to hear Did you know better than to ask certain questions How has marrying a survivor impacted on your life What adjustments have you made Is your spouse particularly demanding Have you had to work very hard to preserve your spouse's fragile equilibrium How often have you put his needs before yours Did you relinquish any old pleasures and traditions that made your spouse uncomfortable Is there anything you wish you hadn't sacrificed Did you have children together Did your spouse worry her past might damage your children Did you discuss whether to tell your children about the holocaust How did your spouse react when the subject came up unexpectedly Did you discourage probing by your children that could distress your spouse Have any of your children been particularly interested in your spouse's experiences during the holocaust How has your spouse dealt with this How have you dealt with this Have you had to put your spouse's needs before the needs of your children Have any of your children been persistent Have any of them dealt with the holocaust in therapy Have any of your children gone through periods of involvement with holocaust groups or conferences Has your spouse Have you Have there been significant changes over the years Has your spouse's reaction to your children's probing changed Has your spouse become more open How have you responded to this change Did it take some of the pressure off Are you grateful that your children rattled the silence   ?

hitler,

    I'm glad you aren't here to gloat about all your new
followers. Sorry you didn't live to be brutally punished. Wish
I believed in hell and could picture you there.

    I'm working to make the world change in ways that would
make you squirm. Going to get pregnant, have a thousand Jewish
babies, swarms and swarms   of Jewish great-grandchildren

PILLOW FIRMLY

My friend's baby
he cried so loud

I couldn't help imagining
what if we were in hiding

I
just
couldn't
help
it

TWO HEADS

Our people say
we - *the generation after* -
must remember; if not
history will repeat itself
against us
or against our children   pinned under
It falls to us:
the world must never forget

Sanctuary
for family past and future, we
must tell
retell:
keep the truth alive and aloud

                                                     impostors

            Living as though
            we are survivors

The survivors say
we replace the lives that were seized,
our relatives
our people
Named after two murdered:
I am a buoy thrown   double crossed
to the drowned

The holocaust
seized our lives too

Living as though
we were victims

                                disguised

The generation after must
live fully
live fruitfully   underpinned
Sometimes we manage grateful,
graceful lives Other times
we barely endure   riddled with fault lines

As shields
we can fail: blows strike us, our children,
others

    Wound tight as cable,
    and split Our two heads
    pulling

Wall of Names, Umschlagplatz, Warsaw, 1993

QUESTIONNAIRE
HOLOCAUST DEAD

What do you want from me Do you wonder if you can appease me How can I appease you Do you see that I have made myself into a guest house, always welcoming, never turning you away Do you hear me rehearsing what you might have said, carrying your words, as many as I can imagine, in my mouth, brimful and spilling Do you know how I marvel at the life of you, your ability to power us, inhabit our being Must we engage in a battle of wills How can we measure who clings hardest, who pushes away Should I join you Do you want to be freed from the living, from dragging around and around on the conveyor belts of our tortured souls When we are thinking of you, what happens When we do not hold you, what then Are you nothing without us Did you plant us here like footprints, guardians, seeds Do the dead change their minds Might you not want the same thing tomorrow Are the living as impossible to predict Will you always love us Do you fear our desertion Do you forgive us Are you merciful Do you want to push us past your murders to know the lives you lived before Do you want to direct us into the lives you never finished Do you want to coax us into lives of our own Are you waiting for us, beckoning, anxious for attention Do you want us to volunteer, resist, succumb Do you choose us, hunt us down, use us as breadcrumbs to find your way home, to heaven, into our miraculous, churning wombs Must I always let you in Let you Always Crumbs mercy

love   Have I   Have I not   Minds carry change spill
No lull no plan Cling rush battle Are you are you only
as real as I can make you Am I as real as you make me
If I push you away, will I stand alone alone, empty in
your place   ?

POSTCARD TO THE HOLOCAUST

dear dad,

      when I was born, you and mom chose for me
your grandmother's name and your mother's name too.
when you set me and my name to sail on the roiling sea,
what did you expect? what did you want for me   from me?
what was it you needed, thundering fists of waves
be damned?

WHAT THE HOLOCAUST SURVIVOR'S DAUGHTER . . .

The delays create considerable anxiety in Berlin, because the liquidation of the ghettos is proceeding apace and the transports are being loaded. The head of the building administration in Berlin writes urgently to Auschwitz, "I know that you have some problems, but you really have to do everything to get the stuff finished and please keep me posted day by day, week by week, of what is happening."

A week later, he is given a memorandum about the electricity, signed by a representative of *AEG*, the major German electricity company, which is creating the installation. The memorandum concerns the use of the available machines with the current electricity supply to the cremetoria which makes possible "burning with simultaneous Special Treatment."

Not only Topf, the makers of the ovens, not only the builders are involved, but also one of the major German electricity companies, *AEG*, which has a very prosperous existence in the Federal Republic today. Finally the crematoria are finished and handed over to the SS. Birkenau is fully operational. Poison gas and crematoria technology have been deliberately combined to create a mechanism of mass murder.

The final report states, "In Crematorium I: 340 people can be incinerated every 24 hours, and in numbers II and III: 1440, and in Crematorium IV and V: 768. There is a daily incineration capacity in Auschwitz of 4756 persons." *

* *Adapted from interview of Robert Jan Van Pelt, Professor of Architecture, in documentary film "Nazi Designers of Death," a NOVA, BBC, WGBH, production, 1995.*

AEG Oko-Lavamat 508
The Environment-Friendly Washing Machine
Operating Instructions:
Hello

Allow me to introduce myself:
I am your AEG Oko-Lavamat environment-friendly
automatic washing machine.
From now on, I should like to make washing
easier for you, and not simply because of my
attractive appearance, but also thanks to my
"Intrinsic Qualities".

I am economical in terms of energy, water, and
detergent consumption, especially quiet in
operation, easy to operate, and simple to care for.

If you carefully read and follow my operating
instructions before first use and familiarize
yourself with my installation and connection
instructions, you are sure to experience a good
deal of joy when using me to wash your laundry!

Made in Germany
Printed on recycled paper

AEG - Putting Words Into Action
Appliance Packaging Information:
All materials used are environmentally compatible.
They can be safely disposed of or
burnt in a refuse incinerator. **

** *Quoted from the "AEG Oko Lavamat 508 Operation Manual," 1991.*

POSTCARD TO THE HOLOCAUST

dear family,

   maybe you weren't even the kind of people I would want to know maybe you would have been the kind of relatives I would ignore maybe you wouldn't have liked me maybe emigration would have separated us. maybe I don't even have enough information to imagine you maybe we would have had birthdays together maybe we would have been close maybe I'd have married a cousin. maybe if it weren't for hitler   my parents would never have met I would never have been born maybe I wouldn't torment dwelling on how your murders are wedged into my birth and maybe I shouldn't lament lots of births come from sorry circumstances but we'll never get to talk about it and who knows what we'd say anyhow me shouting through deepening layers to you located somewhere in my thrashing marrow   almost safe within my ambivalent bones

"JEWISH GRAVES DESECRATED IN FRANCE"

What did those graves do
to attract attention to themselves?
I worry

I might (fatally)
do the same

SENSING ABSENCE

(i)

When a holocaust survivor dies a natural death,
even if strained, even if peaceful,
our collective souls
pause.

Perhaps in an apartment,
a retirement home, the hospital, a bed.
With loved ones, or even alone.

Perhaps the body is in control
or the mind, or both,
or none.
Perhaps he is willing.
Perhaps she fights.

Not murder. Death.
One
at a time.

(ii)

When a holocaust survivor is buried,
a cotton shroud, a wooden casket.

Hear the sound of shoveled earth
falling. Music:

dirt on wood, dirt on dirt,
grass on dirt, and a stone,
soon her own headstone.
A survivor's flame
etched in the corner.

And people will visit. Mourners
will step soft and slow
on the kept grass. Jostle
little stones in hand,
leave them to settle
like warm beach sand.

(iii)

When a survivor comes to a funeral,
her sadness swells like no other:
impossible
to know for whom, how many
the sorrow.

Absence stirs,
flurry of rushing wings.

(iv)

Come to a still cemetery
memorial tombs and plaques and individual graves stand
and there are trees and paths and flowers,
a look of permanence.

Here to stay.

Here to bring memories
home.

POSTCARD TO THE HOLOCAUST

dear holocaust survivor,

you and me both asking and asking, what, oh what, would you have been like without the war?

what difference did it make? tell me who you might have been. and the rest of us, the rest of us, would we be so frightened always?

Henia and Henryk's grave, New Jewish Cemetery (established 1800), Cracow, 1996

Travelling

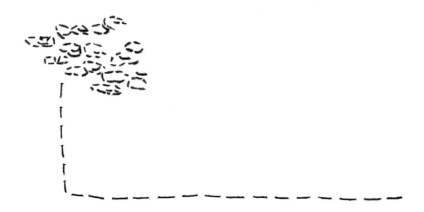

WHO SPEAKS. WHO IS SILENT.

Who speaks.   Who is silent.
Who aims the camera.   Who looks away.
Who records history.   Who is recorded.
Who are the perpetrators.   Who are the victims.
Who frames the photograph.   Who is framed.
Who controls.   Who pleads.
Who murders.   Who is killed.
Who denies.   Who remembers.
Who has the last word.

Whose photographs occupy the walls of our museums.

                                                                Imagine

                                                    the photographs

                                                    we will never see.

Inspired by artist Barbara Kruger.

TRAVELLING IN THE DEAD OF FALL

Winter:

the ground there is white,
shrill,
barbed.

> *There is no way I will ever go to Poland.*

Spring:

growth presses downward,
and upward
from beneath.

> *Now, we are considering the possibility.*

Summer:

roots pierce.
petals grasp
coloured light.

> *My father will not return.*
> *We may go on our own.*

Fall:

roots knot in the crowded earth.
petals drop
into mosaics.

> *We will go in September.*

POLAND: A RETURN IN FIVE VOICES

Ruth speaks: *Grandmother, I will be there*

That I can do this now
when before I couldn't:
That we have booked our tickets
and planned our travels
several times, and this one
final:
I will be there.

We will plant seeds
I have culled from my own garden,
around my grandmother's grave
and blanket them with wire mesh.

The cosmos we sow
into the old cemetery earth
will win over year by year the weeds,
defy year by year our absence,
spread year by year across this land,
where not even our gravestones
are let remain standing.

Raymond speaks: *My daughter, my mother*

I will never forget the blue of my mother's dead face.
I have not cried since I was made to kiss it.
My daughter Ruth insists, so I will choose some stones.

Henia speaks: *Granddaughter, our distance for a moment will rest*

She does not know if once I gardened.
She does not know if I love flowers.
She does not know.

She brings seeds from her home
and little stones from the home of
her father,
my son.

      Our distance.

The little stones
she will handle and place
upon my gravestone.

The seeds, she will protect
in the earth around me. My breath
will be their sun.

Their flowers, my lungs.

A Polish echo speaks: *There*

What's she doing in there, the girl, digging about
the rubble. Cemetery's in the way of construction.
They won't move it 'cause the Jews will complain. Jews,
controlling what we Poles do. Memorials everywhere.
Good for business. Money-makers
even when they're dead.

We speak: *Our presence*

Years later,
Poland overrun.
Blue white yellow fuchsia orange red,
rampant
cosmos.

יודאיקה בפולין

JUDAICA W POLSCE • JUDAICS IN POLAND

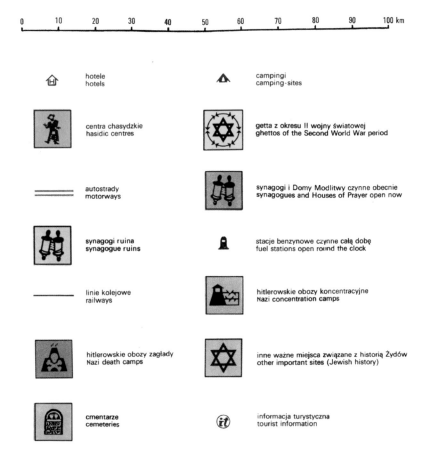

hotele / hotels	**campingi** / camping-sites
centra chasydzkie / hasidic centres	**getta z okresu II wojny światowej** / ghettos of the Second World War period
autostrady / motorways	**synagogi i Domy Modlitwy czynne obecnie** / synagogues and Houses of Prayer open now
synagogi ruina / synagogue ruins	**stacje benzynowe czynne całą dobę** / fuel stations open round the clock
linie kolejowe / railways	**hitlerowskie obozy koncentracyjne** / Nazi concentration camps
hitlerowskie obozy zagłady / Nazi death camps	**inne ważne miejsca związane z historią Żydów** / other important sites (Jewish history)
cmentarze / cemeteries	**informacja turystyczna** / tourist information

Adapted from "Judaics In Poland" map, produced in 1991 by Centur Publishers of the Polish Tourist Information Centre, funded by the State Office for Sport and Tourism

Pond at Birkenau, 1993

VISITING THE POND AT BIRKENAU DEATH CAMP

What I know :

The pond has not always looked like this.
It was once murky
with the ashes
of people.
The pond did not always look like that.
Before then
it was just a pretty pond.

The pond is not large.
Bodies burn down to very little. Picture an urn
its small treasure of ash. Very small
plus very small   plus very small. Not one by one
but by the cart load   as the ashes collected
beneath the ovens : from the ovens to the pond   from the ovens
to the pond   from the ovens

The grass around my feet reveals no trace of the carts' wheels
no light footsteps of the bony inmates
who pushed them : what a path they must have worn
these pallbearers of ash.
Broken posts in the water   remains of a platform
where the carts dumped the ashes   greying the water
in circles : and the water
always able to receive more.

To know
so many deaths fit into this small pond.
To see
the pond has recovered so fully.

Too benign. I know not to turn my back on it.

There is nothing to see :

There is nothing to see.

This is just a pond. Without the sign
we wouldn't even have known.
There is nothing   nothing   that gives it away.

So we stand there. Waiting.

Waiting for the pond.
For the pond to betray itself.
It just lies there
beautiful.

Waiting
for the pond to falter
to show us what we came to see
fearing. What we came to see:
What it looked like
How it happened
Did the ashes resist
and stay afloat?

What dares grow here now?
Wildflowers   pine trees   grass
pine cones I collect as mementos.
A farmer has ridden on his bicycle to pick mushrooms.

We take photographs   close ups   hoping
to enlarge them later and look
closely. Surely they would reveal

I hold them now
like the pond   the photographs
release nothing.

For there is nothing on the water   nothing
in the grass   nothing in the sky
nothing to see.

Blessed

nothing.

CUT FROM THE LIVING

Hair, cut from the living and the dead,
combed, cleaned and packed by inmates' hands,
weighed, inventoried and shipped to factories,
hair worked into thread and felt,
socks for submarine crews and railroad workers,
ropes and cords for ships,
stuffing for mattresses and pillows,
haircloth for igniting bombs

At Auschwitz

I let a curling strand of my own hair
flicker to the grass
wind a burial shroud around
each blade, around
the barracks, fences, towers crowded
with the ever-present slayers, bring
them, bring them crashing down

CRACOW NOW

My father
never saw the pattern
on the ten bales of cloth
his parents traded for his life.

When I stood on the corner in Cracow
where the trade took place
I pictured the handoff, the relief
greed had been sated.

I placed a flower
on the window ledge.
My self: proof, rebuke, belated
witness. Warp, weft,
thread.

The corner where the extortion took place, Cracow, 1993

ŁASKAWI PAŃSTWO

Wiadomym jest powszechnie, że robiliście konszachty i różne
interesy z Żydami. (Co jest zakazane). Mieliście na przechowaniu
żydówkę M. z jej małym synem, za co grozi kara śmierci.

P. Otto robił interesy ze swoim sąsiadem sklepowym żydem Kuba.
Wynika z tego, że rodzina Pradłów jak równie rodzina synowej
wyraźnie sympatyzuje z tą „wybrana rasa" i to tym bardziej jeszcze
bo przechowuje rzeczy żydowskie!! Jest tych rzeczy dużo, żeby
odstąpić drugiej osobie „do przechowania"

DAJCIE do przechowania część /minimum 10 kujnow dobrego
gatunku - nie szmaty/ materiałów żydówki M. A co do Kuby
to sprawę zostawiam w spokoju!"

Czekam na odbiór tego dużego pakunku w poniedziałek
dn. 1.III 43 na rogu ul. Mogilskiej a ul. Lubomirskiej o godzinie
6tej (18) wieczorem.

PRZYJACIEL

P.S. NIE próbójcie wynieść rzeczy z domu bo na wszystko
mam dowody i Kasprowicz jak Żyblikiewicz ulice są pod nasza
obserwcją.

Adres żydówki jest ul. F. i dowód najlepszy.

Extortion letter delivered to Mechel and Henia, Cracow, winter, 1943

DEAR SIRS

It is commonly known that you have colluded with and done business with Jews (which is forbidden). You were hiding a young jewess M. and her small son, which is punishable by death.

Mr. Otto was making all kinds of deals with the jew Kuba who runs the neighbouring shop.

It is evident from this that both the Pradlow family and your son's wife's family sympathise with this "chosen race," particularly so since they are storing jewish property!! There is a lot of this property, so some of it could be passed over to another person "for safe-keeping"

GIVE me a part for storage (a minimum of 10 bales of good quality cloth - not rags) of the materials of the Jewess M. And as far as Kuba is concerned, I will leave this matter in peace!!

I will be waiting to take delivery of this big package on Monday 1st March 1943 on the corner of Mogilska St. and Lubomirska St. at 6pm (18) hours.

A FRIEND

P.S. DO NOT try to remove those things from the house because I have evidence for everything and both Kasprowicz and Zyblikiewicz Streets are being watched by us.
The address of the jewess is street F. and that's the best proof.

Translation of extortion letter.

Looking for the apartment of hiding, Cracow, 1993

POSTCARD TO THE HOLOCAUST

dear janina,

    You used to buy cloth in my grandfather's store, before the war, before the Germans decreed all Jews must live in the ghetto. My grandparents did not obey. How did they come to hide in your apartment? Did they knock at your door? How did they ask? What did you say?

    We have no words.

    Did you like them? Had they helped you before? Did you need the money, the single American dollars my grandfather rolled into a condom, hid in his buttocks and in the mattress, losing some once to a gnawing rat whose feast might have cost them their lives. (This instance of incisive anguish is one of the few moments my father remembers, as if the razor of that loss passes now across his throat.) Did my grandmother care for your baby when you went to work? Were you angry at the occupation and wanting to fight back?

    We have no reasons.

    What was it like? What went through your mind? How did you feed yourselves? Were you afraid? How did it feel to visit the library every day to bring books for my father? What happened at night? Did neighbours notice and demand payoff? Did you ever want to change your mind? How did my grandparents dissuade you? What did you do to protect yourselves?

    We have no pictures.

Were you Volksdeutch, as my father thinks, Polish but German, too, with status above the Poles – extra rations, permission to keep your apartment, a job? Is it true you had relations with a German police or *SS* man, who pinned his card to your apartment door, claiming you and signalling to the Polish police to pass without searching? That when he stayed over, my grandparents and my father would hide behind the springs of a mattress stored upright in the closet? That he came once when you were not home and, very drunk, searched for you, poking his gun into the mattress and teasing lewdly?

We have no sounds.

After the war, did my grandparents ever visit? You died only eight years later, at forty-two. Did you know that after your death, my grandfather sent American dollars to your daughter Elzbieta? And after his death, my family continues. I visited Poland this fall and met your daughter. She is fifty-four now. We took her to lunch in a café on the main square and to the building where she thought you had lived during the war, trying to find the apartment. But Elzbieta was ten years old when you died, still too young to pass the story down. Later, in the room where she lives, we gave her money to buy a longed for television and took her photograph: she is holding a coveted snapshot of herself in her wheelchair, being blessed by the Pope.

We will always assist her.

You see, Janina, I am trying to sit us down together, ask *Why did you hide them?* I want to list your virtues, as if an explanation would elevate you, and make us more worthy. As if an answer would move me like a chorus, and I would stop everything to listen my way to a gracious, sustaining place.

WALTZ-LIKE, STEPHAN DANCED

Waltz-like, Stephan danced the story
Of Nika's family's hiding
No shared aural language between us

Where they crept down
How small the coal cellar
How they crouched day night day night day

How neighbours betrayed them to Fascist partisans
How the partisans tortured the father of the family hiding them
How his children would be tortured too if he didn't point the way

How Pola, Ignatz, Moniek, Salek, Moisze, Chamek were torn out torn apart
Forced to remove all their clothes onto the snow
Told to run across the field toward the small forest valley

How the parents clutched their children and ran
How the partisans shot them and laughed
How the children fell from their arms

How the partisans shot them too
Children little children little little
Stephen's hand showing their height

Just one day before the end of the war
As if that heightens the tragedy
And it does

As if time's betrayal deepens human betrayal
As if adult betrayal of children compounds evil
As if betrayal by neighbours heightens treachery

And it does
Waltz-like, Czieslava moved behind him
Unconsciously pantomiming too

Waltz-like, we traced with him
The motions of their terror
Stopping before they would be killed again

With our fingers
Stephan, Czieslava and I rolled back the grass
Dug up the eroded stone step

We planted bulbs in a ring
Lit a candle at their centre
Entwined our hands to protect it from the wind

In Zagorzany, Poland, the farm that once belonged to the Catholic Czieslava's widowed father now belongs to Czieslava and her husband, Stephan. Her father helped twelve of Nika's family - sisters, brothers, their spouses, their children - hide in the coal cellar under his barn.

Stephan and Czieslava mime the story of Nika Mandel's family's hiding, Zagorzany, 1993

TIME CAPSULE

The objects go in easily
but the papers have to be folded, refolded, unfolded,
refolded
before they will fit
As though they want to be handled
blessed with my touch
before their descent

Behind Grandmother Henia and Uncle Henryk's grave
my husband Ian digs the hole
With the panic of finality
we close our time capsule
a blue plastic thermos
entrusted with mementos

I lay the time capsule
in their earth

a treasure chest

Some things for Uncle Henryk to play
only nine when he was murdered
Cracow crowded with death

       Kids don't grow up once they've been killed
       even when many years pass

a lock of my hair

Jewish hair
long, dark and curling
Not stuffed into German pillows
Not woven into German cloth
This hair is loose, decorated, shimmering
A plume

an invitation to my wedding

I married Ian, who is not Jewish, and
wonder if
my father is relieved
thinking I am safer
          Even if history has shown
          I endanger another

a photograph of our dog

My hawk-eyes watch her
in daytime when she plays alone in the yard
and at night when in my nightmares
she is skinned, beaten, terrorized, stolen
          I wake knotted
          contemplate removing the mezuzah
          from our front door

two poems I have written

We made our final decision to go to Poland
visiting relatives I had never met
dear relatives
fifty years dead

> Set my poems
> among these graves
> among those I write about

> A web of words
> between us

family photographs from before the war

My favourite, the one where
my father and his brother Henryk lean
against their mother Henia
tall flowers behind them
looks like they are playing
relaxed smiles
my father and his brother
all sweetness in their suspendered shorts
and the sun on their forearms
each resting a small loyal hand
on their mother's knee

> Listen to me going on
> as if I can *detail* them
> back to life

Some people
you can't visit
even if you miss them hard
even if they seem no longer dead

seeds we have planted

From my home
into the earth around them
                breath sun flowers lungs
Into the capsule
                sealed dry dark preserved
                their potential always within

a photograph from my wedding

Look
that's me in the middle
and my husband
Starting on the left
that's my older brother, my younger brother
then my father, my mother
her mother, her father, her sister
and on the right, that's my step-grandmother Nika
who Zaidi married wanting a mother for his son
There we all are

           Photographs can't bridge the gap

           Defiant hands press through fifty years
           place fingertips

under our chins
studiously raise our faces to a better angle
tilt them to and fro
for a better look

a piece of rock from Zakopane

From the fresh mountain air
a fist-sized rock
we broke into pieces
one for me, one for each brother, one for dad and mom
one for the capsule
Rock from Zakopane
where dad went after the war to recover his health

> *Recover*
> must not be the right word
> since all these years later
> there I was, the same spot, tears still running

a pine cone from Zakopane

The sun the trees their seeding cones
because nature doesn't stop for genocide
Keeps evolving
takes with it the decomposing dead
leaves us behind

our family tree

> The table in our home is never set for many
> and you should see how funny our family tree looks
> all wide across the top
>
> My father
> a single branch dangling
> from his generation
>
> My brothers and I
> dangling
> from my father

and little stones from our homes in Toronto

> The time capsule, a clutch
> of little stones
> I settle
> within

With all our love and company

> Our distance for a moment
> rests

Placed on Yom Kippur, Saturday September 25, 1993, at the grave of Henia and Henryk Mandel, the New Jewish Cemetery in Cracow, Poland.

Preparing to tend Henia and Henryk's grave, New Jewish Cemetery, Cracow, 1993

POSTCARD TO THE HOLOCAUST

dear uncle henryk,

      I was told you were killed by friends trusted to hide you
but in the cemetery in Cracow I saw the gravestone you share with
your mother engraved "Henryka Mandla Born January 21 1933
Transported August 1942 to Belzec"   there is no one to tell us
what is true you must answer *How were you killed?* we need to
know   memory's story needs a vanishing point or it lingers leaves us
asking when what we want is to say   *It happened like this*

Henryk Mandel, 1939

POSTCARD TO THE HOLOCAUST

whoever you are,

were you the last person to hurt my uncle Henryk? was it you who killed him? are you still alive? can I come to your town and watch you hobble about your garden? will my presence unsettle you? will you avoid my questions and busy yourself digging? will you throw down your spade and charge away?

can I follow you into your home and tell your great-grandchildren what you and I know? what will their small hands feel the next time you touch them? will they begin to wish, as I do, that until you become dust, every child's face inflicts on you a millennium of remorse

EXCAVATING THE HOLOCAUST

Dredging the pond
back into ashes back
into embers back
into suffocated bodies back
into lungs back
into shorn and stripped hundreds back
into herded lines back
onto trains
back
into the familiar hum of cities

Bullet holes in walls
back into blood-stains back
into pierced bodies back
into bullets back
into round-ups
back
into Jewish families
and the families who tried to hide them

Chalky white dust
back into thick plaster back
into crushed fetuses back
into fertile women back
into full wombs
back
into warm hands cradling lush bellies

Gold
back into teeth back
into jaws back
into mouths back
into voices
back
into the criss-crossing rise and fall of chatter

Dark green weeds
back into soil back
into compost back
into bones back
into flesh back
into gestures
back
into the brisk crowds of market day

Rough rags and pressed pillows
back into muffled cries back
into babies
back
into the children they would have become
back
into the children they would have born

We would be safe then
and unclench our stomachs
speak yiddish
have cousins

visit the homes our adept imaginations
reel in
from the past.

Henia, Mechel, Henryk Mandel, Cracow, 1939

POSTCARD TO THE HOLOCAUST

dear reader,

     some families boast of a condo in florida time share in
barbados cottage on a lake places they take pride in pine for dream
of for comfort I don't envy them a thing   Us   we have a grave in
poland yes we do resting place of my grandmother henia also
dedicated to my uncle henryk both killed in the Shoah   oh don't
underrate our good fortune we're the envy of many most people
have nowhere to tend nowhere to visit just camps that have been
razed to the ground pits covered over with roads or swallowed by
farmers' fields old addresses with new residents looking at you
sideways some people borrow a grave ask if they can pray there
a stand in for what they don't have   not Us   we have a grave in
poland   I was there this very fall tending and digging planting and
weeping took pictures for when I came home it's there on the wall
when I need it   precious

QUESTIONNAIRE
CHILDREN OF SURVIVORS

Name Who are you named after Who do you resemble Who do you replace Whose life Whose body Whose skin Do you ever want to ask Do you ever not want to hear Do you ever wish they would stop telling Wish they would start Are you protective of your parents Are you allowed to ask questions about their experiences Are some things prohibited Do you ever tell others Do you wish you hadn't Do you feel relief Is so much information missing that it's impossible to piece together Is information withheld or unknown Which stories hurt most Which details Which silences Do you ever go numb or try to Do you ever find yourself crying uncontrollably Do you feel guilty when you are sad or happy or misbehave Do you have to remind yourself it was not your fault Do you experience feelings that seem to belong to someone else Do you know whose memories inhabit you Whose conscience Whose nightmares play over and over The ones that end with barbs in your skin The ones that last all night What feelings trouble you most Are you prone to negativity and distrust What feelings serve you well Whose perseverance Whose spirit Do you empathize easily Do you have bull's-eye intuition Do you have an irksome sense that you are on loan from the past, or borrowed from the future For whom do you live According to whose dreams Whose desires Whose prayers Do you make excuses for your existence Do you have feelings of inadequacy, resentment or remorse

Do you dislike questionnaires like this and feel none of this applies to you Does the holocaust manifest as a steel chain rusting in your gut Do you worry more than is comfortable Do you ever wish you could just turn it off Do you double check the front door lock Do you panic when the phone rings at an odd hour Do you ride the brakes Do you make endless back up plans If *this* happens, then do *that* If *that* happens, then do *this* Do you always keep an eye on the lookout for trouble Do you make note of exits and possible escape routes What one recurring thought or image do you wish you could stop forever What event do you fear above all else What do you do to prevent it How will you know when it's too dangerous Do you anticipate when you would flee Do you worry about where you would go and what you would take Who you would leave behind Do you think you could survive   ?

POSTCARD TO THE HOLOCAUST

dear ian,

Our lenses so different, we see different worlds. Our discord and our harmony – the careful, rigorous architecture of our lives.

The First International Gathering of Children Hidden During World War II in New York City. You were unequivocal. I announced to my parents, "Ian and I are going to the conference. Join us if you want." And they did.

After registration, we four, in the hotel café, conference name tags glinting from every bustling table. Floodgates straining. You ask Dad a question about the holocaust. Mom and I do not breathe.

Dad dives in. Dad dives into each question, answers in long, long strokes. Recollection upon recollection. Huddling below the windowsill, not to be seen from the street, face toward sun, to catch some colour, not look so pale, so hidden, so prey. Roaming dark streets alone, when his harrowed parents became convinced their hiding place would be discovered that night. Convinced he would be safer outside, safer alone. Warned not to return until daybreak, until he could see no German police, no Polish police, or never return, if he saw danger. Keep walking, walking. After the war, fierce bronchitis, sent with Erna to the mountains of Zakopane for the air. Later, his favorite pool in Cracow, regaining strength, length upon length.

Mom and I do not breathe. Afraid Dad will stumble. Afraid we might flinch. Scared for each other and ourselves. No stopping him.

Nor you. Ravenous, spellbound. We want to hear, even if it will change us forever.

Dad unfolded piecemeal a map, invited us to look. And we looked. We would not refold, until we explored for ourselves. I would never have gone to Poland without you.

Never. I remember exactly: You helped me put myself on the plane to Poland, took me by the hand, guided me coaxed me dragged me off the plane, onto the bus, into Warsaw, into the hotel, back out again, to expose myself to Poland, let Poland see me. Dread and dare.

In Cracow, we found Dad's pool, climbed down its deep, parched emptiness and pretended to front crawl over faded blue cracks, dusty weeds and shrubs. We searched for the apartments where Dad had lived, where he had hidden. Kindly, unsure occupants let us sit inside. We meandered the streets, with and without our maps. Rode the very same cable car, outrageously vintage, up the highest mountain in Zakopane and hiked down its steep rivers of rocks.

Roving Commemorators, we called ourselves, pink and purple flowers always in hand to imprint our stops. One bright declaration pressed to each family landmark. You take pictures to give. And so do I.

Our lenses so different

Roman's favourite swimming pool, Cracow, 1993

THE HOLOCAUST IS

Not a metaphor
not an allegory
not a symbol

Not a stage
not a backdrop
not a mood

Not an example
not a measure
not *the worst*

The holocaust is not is not is not

Not a syringe through which you inject *meaning*
not a train for you to ride on
not a camp
where you can play

Not an accessory
those who survived have nothing left but the word
and you would wear it for *effect*
no, it is not for dress up

The holocaust is
smell   sound   sight
a scream without end
ringing   and ringing   and ringing

the holocaust is
the holocaust is
the holocaust is

R.12

CANADIAN PACIFIC RAILWAY
DEPARTMENT OF IMMIGRATION AND COLONIZATION
IDENTIFICATION CARD

Date of Issue *17th June 1949* Serial No. *P8671*

The Bearer *MANDEL MICHEL* of *POLAND*

       Family name first, in block letters   Country of origin.

accompanied by his family consisting of **3** *souls is proceeding*

                                 Number

on S.S. **Scythia** *sailing from* **Havre** *on July 16, 1949*

                                            Date

and has been approved for land settlement subject to visa at Embarkation Port.

    Emma Donald **C. L. NORWOOD.**

Emigrant is going forward to Mr. **CANADIAN PACIFIC RAILWAY Co.**

                At **215, ST. JAMES STREET WEST.**

                         MONTREAL. [OVER

IDENTIFICATION CARD.

This card is issued to identify emigrant at point of debarkation and will be retained by the emigrant until finally ticketed to destination, at which time it will be lifted by the Representative of the Department of Immigration and Colonization. This Identification Card to be inserted in cover and carried with passport.

COLONIST SPEAKS THE FOLLOWING LANGUAGE(S)

Polish German English

[signature]

_____

Signature of emigrant for identification.

                                    [OVER

Mechel Mandel's Identification Card, issued by Canadian Department
of Immigration and Colonization, 1949

Who Speaks

SKIN

Let me tell you a story about loss.

*O*nce upon a time there was a loss so complete it peeled
the skin off the hearts of an entire people. A loss so deep
that for years everyone was afraid to use their blood.

Time passed impotently as no one dared ask nor utter nor
evoke. Many years were spent living from the head up, hiding
and protecting furiously pulsing hearts. Many years were
spent fearfully pretending that many years could go on this way.

But everyone knew one day children would be born, children
who would not want to live without their flesh.

*E*ventually these children were conceived, the unions of
skinned histories, carried with joy and hope, held in wombs
churning with suspense.

And one day these children were born. Born kicking, born
frightened, born into the plot of stories untold. Clasped shut.

*A*s these children grew up they didn't dare ask or utter or evoke.
But their dreams were visited by soulful shadows and their days
were stalked by restless tears.

No longer children, they refused to live with skinless hearts
and blood stilled in their veins.

*T*hey began to kick, as when they were born.

Roman and Mechel Mandel, Cracow, 1947

dear zaidi mechel,

You must have been able to see through our thin, awkward synagogue charade, pretending we were going, pretending we had been. You played your part, never risked more than a simple question, answerable with an eyes-averted nod, "This morning you went to the Holy Blossom, yes?" You never tried to trick us.

At the time, I wondered, why Mom and Dad didn't just blurt the truth and stop the charade, assert with an angled, stiff hand slicing the air, "We're not going, not interested. Neither are the kids."

You loved to sing from the bimah at your synagogue. Your beautiful voice belonged there, settled, partly at home, partly longing. Maybe this was a surprise even to you, so willfully urban before the war, so modern, rejecting your father's violent push toward rabbinic school. How our parents infiltrate us. Our grandparents too.

We children fought for ham sandwiches on white bread and got them without much fuss. That wasn't what Mom and Dad cared about, though it may have sorrowed you. They had to choose their fronts. Going to synagogue mattered to you. Dad knew young, and Mom must have learned from him, to play along. Thirty anguished years after the war, they did not want to cause you to suffer any more regrets. It was that, wasn't it. Continuity in obvious forms was missing.

It would be years before we children could focus any of the faces that stared with us into the mirror, clamouring to see a bit of themselves in us. Long years before we would recognize what had shone through from one generation to the next, to glimpse you in us. And it would not necessarily be what you strove to send through. Not what you expected at all. We can never know exactly what we will perpetuate, can we? Zaidi, don't despair, the revealing is incremental, ongoing. You have to keep watch.

Which reminds me, after you died, your friend gave us a tape of you singing the Rosh Chodesh prayer for the new month. Maybe you remember her holding the tape recorder up to your mouth, leaning into the tiny square microphone. My brother David incorporated your song into his music. Cleared up the hiss and static as best he could. Mixed and remixed. Your voice, clear and resonant, holds your prayer aloft at the front of his song, "Wisdom Cries."

Who'd have thought? Really. And isn't that the point of it all? The long wait. The surprise. We can't know what it means exactly, what he has done, your grandson David, sending your voice out to the radio world. You, to whom we did and did not listen. Your prayer, via David, rocking our world.

In loving memory of Mechel Mandel — June 21, 1906 - February 5, 1985

FAMILY THERAPY

is great
I recommend it
if you ever get a chance to try it
it's killer but really worth it
even when you're older
which we were
our therapist is a child of survivors too
so she knows what we went through as kids
as parents as a family
and didn't cringe
at the grueling scenes or shy away
from the tormented relationships
that spiral out of war and trauma

We were just wrapping up one session
around the middle of the process
we had covered what my dad went through
at the end of the war
which he describes as the beginning
for him of another war of sorts
that smashed away at what was left
of his sparse reconfigured family

They remained in Poland briefly
and then emigrated
fled really to Paris then Toronto
he talked about his father and new stepmother
and other relatives what they were like
to him and to each other

really inconsistent tumultuous
everything a phenomenal mess
and nobody the least bit okay
but they were trying to re-assemble
barely plugging along
he was ten or eleven years old
dead brother dead mother dead grandparents
dead cousins dead friends
trying to keep up with not much help
and hardly any sympathy

After we heard all this
for the first time ever
my brothers and I and my mother
were sniffling away and scraping
ourselves off the floor
when my dad
perks up and throws out
"You know, all this, all this, it didn't affect me"

"Dad"
I looked him in the eyes
"it's lucky it didn't affect you
because if it had
it would have been
devastating"

Inside the hiding apartment, Apartment 9, 4 Rakovicka Street, Cracow,
Ray's writing marks the "original door to walk in closet," 1996

CAPTIVE CHILD

If I were a child in the holocaust
I would wonder why I had to hide here,
in this stranger's apartment, in this closet,
between the springs of this mattress.

       I would be so scared.

I would want to sleep in my own bed.
I would wish my older brother Henryk had not hit me.
I would wish I had not yelled at him.
I would want someone to bring me candy.

       I would give Henryk three pieces.

I would wish my father had not taken him to hide with a different family.
I would wish that family had kept the promise.
I would wish whoever dragged Henryk away had believed him
when he screamed "I am not a Jew! I am not a Jew!"

       I would want someone to help us.

I would wonder if I will ever see him again now that he is dead.
I would cry and cry and cry.
I would read so many books.
I would want to eat chocolate.

       I would want to play with my brother.

I would want my mother and father to protect me.
I would dream that I could walk to school

and not be beaten up by children,
not be cursed by grown ups and hit by teachers.

I would miss having friends.

I would wish that people would stop telling me to
"Shhh" and "Be quiet" and "Don't cough or we'll all die."
I would dream that no one could laugh or play
or have birthdays or new toys until I could have some too.

I would want to be invisible.

I would think maybe nobody knows this is happening to us.
I would wonder how other people could ignore it,
how they could just go about their daily business
and leave me here hiding forever.

I would want the whole world to stop.

If I were a child in the holocaust
I would want to be on everyone's mind all the time.
I would wish there were no distractions.
I would wish no one could make excuses.

I would want my parents to have their store back.

I would wish no one was selfish.
I would wish no one was too busy.
I would wish that someone watching
would want to save me.

I would never trust anyone.

I would want people to make a big fuss and yell.
I would want everybody to write letters and make phone calls
and devote every second to saving us.
I would want someone important to get us out.

I would want to go home.

I would pretend I was a character in a play.
I would wish for Superman and Wonder Woman and Spiderman.
I would pretend I wasn't hiding for real.
I would wish it would be over soon.

I would want to see someone smile.

I would wait for the good soldiers to come.
I would wish my father could rest.
I would wish my mother could get medicine.
I would want to be allowed to shout and to play and get sick.

I would want to see the sun.

If I were a child in the holocaust
I would want to grow up some day
into someone
I would want
to be.

I write

to loosen the air

around me.

I give this poem,

offer truce.

Captive child,

free me.

all noise running shouting guards bash
me backward sideways forward fear fear
fear in the shape of a line a woman leans
to me whispers *You see that smoke?*
as if that explains something as if that
makes any sense *That's you if you go left!*
as if she is doing me a favour as if if if
there's some connection must be crazy
jostled forward quickly *Right is life!* pulling
at my arm making sure guards don't see
wants me to look look look ahead
a man in white gloves waving his
hand his hand his hand people parting
either side so many people going each way
shesheshe makes no

TRACES

Mommy Mommy Mommy Mommy
Mommy, my toddler's call
rescues me
from a nightmare as she climbs onto our bed.
I say, *Mommy had a bad dream.*
She coos, *Mommy having bad dreams?*
Her eyes dart to my shoulder
she glares
swipes at it with her small hand, *There.*
There's a bad dream. Ziva rub it. Ziva
push it away. Nightmare traces
our children
try to wipe away.

INCANTATION

If I am not for myself
then who will be for me
if I am not for myself
then who am I for
if I am not for myself.

If I am not for my family
then will they stand with me
if I am not for my family
then who am I for
if I am not for my family.

If I am not my own conscience
then whose conscience am I
if I am not my own conscience
then whose conscience will be mine
if I am not my own conscience.

If I do not express my emotions
then whose emotions do I express
if I do not express my emotions
then who will express them for me
if I do not express my emotions.

If I do not interpret this history
then what history will I have
if I do not interpret this history
then who will
if I do not interpret this history.

If I am not living my own life
then whose life am I living.
Father, if I am you
then who
will be me?

QUESTIONNAIRE
CHILD HOLOCAUST SURVIVORS

Current name If known, please provide: Birth name
Name(s) used during the war Parents' names Date of
birth Place of origin Age at the outbreak of war What
did you think when the war began How did your life
begin to change How did your parents react Were they
able to explain anything to you How did you survive
the war Did you hide with parent(s) Did you wander
and hide alone Were you mistreated by the people who
were supposed to protect you Were you converted to
another religion Did you pass as the opposite sex
Were you subjected to experiments Did you travel with
partisans Did you have a special friend who helped
you During the war did you have any contact with
family members Did you have any knowledge of what
was happening to them When did the war end for you
How old were you Do you remember what happened
to you then Did any parent or relative survive the war
Who came to claim you Did you know or recognize
them Did they speak a different language Did you
want to go with them or stay where you were Did this
lead to ongoing conflict Did your war-time family want
you to stay Do you still have contact with them Do
you have reason to believe that you were not returned
to your birth family or have not been told the truth about
your origins Did you learn the fate of all family
members Were you able to return to your home Did
any surviving family die from illness caused by the war
Did your parents ever ask you about your hiding
experience Did you emigrate Were you sponsored by

relatives Did you come alone Were you adopted Were your adoptive parents able to know your true identity Do you talk to anyone about what happened to you during the holocaust How do survivors who were adults during the holocaust respond If you have children, how do they respond Do you have any memories from before the war Do you remember family members who were murdered Your mother Your father Your siblings Do you think about why you survived the holocaust Do the gaps in your knowledge trouble you Of all the things you do not know about your past, what one thing do you wish you could find out, more than any other ?

NIKA BY HEART

We mourned in her lifetime
too   Nika
cleaved by the war

who she once was   what happened
during the war   who
she had become

her unceasing longing
the person she might otherwise
have been   instead

Nika   grave among the living
endured carnage of depression   lure
of suicide

she reached for company
reached for every aid every
relief every chance

and cherished
the days months nothing bad
happened nothing went wrong

a wonder
Nika   grave now
among the dead

never to lose
her loved ones
again

Eulogy, Nika Mandel — January 25, 1915 - September 3, 1995

Nika (born Traubman) and Mechel Mandel, Zagorzany, 1947

THE FUTURE

The holocaust dared time to end.
The future barely squeaked by,

carried secret in the torn pockets of survivors.
We, the children, are born pregnant,

the dead lodged inside, like shrapnel.
We grow up in the still-warm shadow of the holocaust,

walk in gravity not of our own making. Yet without gravity,
we have nothing to resist, and could crumble.

You-are-the-future, the passing generation says
and sucks us into their collapsing lungs.

We circulate to exhaust the remaining smoke.
But hate holds us.

Hate holds us teetering on a precipice.
We duck away

fearing a future like our past.
If we don't learn the right lessons from history's mistakes,

we will change the wrong elements, pick up the wrong pieces,
drop them later in horror, our hands stained and disbelieving.

History learns more from its mistakes than we do,
never merely repeats. It improves, innovates,

gets more voracious, makes us sorrier the next time.
We back off, tread so carefully, hoard our luck, think of the cost.

We treasure our lives, won't lay them down for a lesson
the world never learned,

no matter the number of *Never Again*s.
We desperately want to let down our guard,

relax into the life cycle and its rounded edges.
But hate hangs over us.

Day and night we startle from bad dreams, pull the quilt tight,
leave only the smallest opening for breath.

But hate hangs us. Hate hangs us over and over.
We stalk the memories of holocaust survivors

grasping for clues: what to watch out for?
what to do now? what to do next time?

Hoping never to have to ask ourselves: what detail have we
forgotten? missed? what else must we know?

Hoping never to need the answers
we absorb ourselves in the act of living.

Just as the victims went about being people.
Each heartbeat a vast, willful rebellion,

giving the murderers every reason,
every opportunity to stop

Inspired by artist Art Spiegleman.

———

THE LAST PRAYER

Each chunk we bite from life is a prayer. Our treasure chest homes,
our love-magnet pets, each meal
we grudgingly make and casually take.
Prayers to life
      let us flourish let us live
      let us stay leave us be let us stay leave us be.
Utterances we muster as we swallow, spurred by a rush,
gratitude and fear. Vehement pleas
      may we preserve what luck we have.

Babies are prayers. Mothering is prayer.
Each tasting kiss, each chattering
diaper change, each worn red sandal putting on pulling off
each rambling invented story, each whispered
convincing promise. The cradles
we make of our voices, rocking rocking
      may this remain just so may we all be here may we
      do this again and again and again tomorrow and for
      ever.

Each rolling, belly to belly nursing, a recitation.
Her milky new breath, when it joins
with mine, a sanctuary
between our mouths.
Our hands, as they flutter together
and apart. Our wondering fingers together
and apart uttering.

From the instant my doctor said, "Yes, finally,
you are pregnant" my hands

grafted themselves to my slow, anxious belly,
how my hands remained steadfastly there while my baby
cracked through me,
how my hands shifted to her soft head
      may we be safe may we be safe may we be safe
      may we be invulnerable.

The back of the hand faces outside: strategic armour.
The palm inside: devoted sentry.
Poised between the precious and the dangerous - between her head
and the table corner, her shoulders
and the stair she faces down, her eyes
and a violent sight.
The cradle
I make of my hands - infinite, furious,
futile.

                 Those mothers, their babies,
                 them too.

I know now what I was afraid of
trying to decide if we should have a child
what the ambivalence and fear warned
what those mothers knew
those mothers forced to stand, collapsing
in long terrified lines.
My baby knows what their babies knew,
babies held in faltering arms, shielded
by mothers' unyielding hands.

What is lighter than the mother's hand
What is heavier than the mother's exhausted arms

What is heavier than the baby urgent with need.
The weight of your child.
The excessive, faultless pull of gravity, a downward
tug I never want to know; after the terrible trains, the father
gone, the baby in her arms for
ever.

And then in the gun point crush
the mother whispers, put your head on my shoulder.
Her hand cups the back of her baby's head,
her wrist at the nape of the neck, cradling.
Crushed in the chamber,
she draws the head inward,
interweaves shoulder chin cheek
tucks her nose into her baby's neck.
She inhales the tart,
moist scent that secrets there.
Her inhalation, a recitation. The rescuing breath,
held in her mouth.

Mothering, there.
Did she hold it deeply,
safely in her striving lungs.
Did she slowly exhale
close to her baby's mouth
a sanctuary.

In the terror of that sealed room, tugging
each other in the gas,
did she make a sudden choice, or
no choice. Instantaneous.

Later
those mothers, their babies,
extracted from the pile.
The mother's stiff, angled fingers
driven through her baby's
hard soft skull,
panic quickening.

The last protection,
not to suffer longer, not to be orphaned for an instant.
What those mothers suddenly knew
what they did. The fingers
loud and silent in their last plea. The hand's unbearable
story.
What they were so afraid of.
What we are so afraid of.
The last prayer.
The last mothering.

POSTCARD TO THE HOLOCAUST

dear carl and david,

     we take it out on each other don't we   blood thick as siblings
bound and different like vein and artery   no sure stepping stones
between us   we hover at the edge   look each other's way   stand back
step forward

     we each listen and don't listen for the hushed keening hear
and don't hear the scratching through the wall probe and don't probe
words missing   three patrollers   none certain which boundary to scale
we brace ourselves pull against each other *Come see from my eyes*
startled by glimpses of sameness

THE SNARE

The day after my first public reading
my father said,
"Y'know, some of your poems have humour in them.
When you're finished writing
holocaust poems, you should write
some funny ones."

I said,
"Dad,
if you wanted me to write
funny poems,
you should have had
a funny life."

        & we laughed giddy and relieved

until the snare tightened

again

OLD BOXES

"I'm German" she blurts, as I emerge from the bathroom stall
after reading my poetry at this women's writing retreat.
She is tall, blond, somewhat gangly, leaning a little too close
and clearly has more to tell me.
"My dad was in Hitler Youth, but I can't ask him about it.
His parents enrolled him. Sometimes I think my grandparents
say anti-semitic things, but I'm not sure and I can't
ask them about it either."

What am I supposed to say? Evidently
this is a disclosure for her. But, really,
who ever wants to hear about another anti-semite?

She continues "We don't talk about it."

"That's hard in a family."

"Yes" she sighs.

"Well, if you can't talk about it in your family,
it's good to find others to talk with" I say warily.

"I thought you might know about Hitler Youth,
the kinds of things they did, that my father
might have done, I sort of think it was like Scouts."

"No, it wasn't like Scouts, no."

"You don't think so?"

Oppressors' kids!
They grow up wide-eyed and naïve,
while victims' kids are born twinned
to suffering and fear.
"There are lots of books on the subject. But
why don't you just ask your father. Books won't tell you
exactly what *he* did."

"I could never ask him. No way. It would be too uncomfortable."

"Well, you just asked me. And it made me uncomfortable.
Why should *I* be uncomfortable and not your father?"

"But you're used to talking about it."

"No, it's miserable and wretched every time.
I just have no choice. I can't pretend nobody was murdered.
Believe me, I'd rather have been born into one of those
cheerful, crowded, cousin-upon-cousin families
who have great big reunions with signs
posted along country roads to get everybody to the right party."

"I think my grandparents might still be anti-semitic" she repeats
in a manner so self-conscious that she seems, ironically,
to be perpetuating a silence
rather than breaking it.

"Why defend *them*? Why not *me*?
Me. I'm who they're talking about. Doesn't that bug you?
Don't you think you should call them on it?"

"It wouldn't feel right" she answers, too quickly.

"Oh yes it would. At least, it would *be* right.
Why not argue, make them feel crummy,
tell them straight out they are wrong.
I know it's hard, who wants to upset grandparents?"
Put them on the spot. Shake them up.
Don't let them go about with their deadly beliefs.
Make them pay. Make them change.

She reverses direction "I don't really mind
not knowing the details. I mean we get along well, y' know?"

"I'm sure you do. It works well for everybody. If nobody
asks questions, nobody has to answer them."
How dare you unleash this vicious subject
and then scramble away?
Afraid of a little conflict? You won't rile your father
or your grandparents, but you will rile me?
"I don't have an easy time of it, why should you?
Anyway, why ask *me*, of all people,
to answer for *them*? It's obscene, don't you think? I won't
make it easy for you. It's not like me
to let anybody off the hook."

"Well I doubt they did anything, anything
really bad" she says nervously.

"What was *bad, really bad, bad enough*, what was *good*?
It's not the point. I'm sure it's taking a lot of courage
for you to talk, but what do you want from *me*? Forgiveness
for not challenging your family? Absolution for them?
It's your past, *you* take responsibility for it.
Don't shove it over to me."

She lets it sink in "I don't think they really want me to know."

"Yah, but do *you* want to know? That's really the question.
You have to go from there. Think about it at least,
why do I have to stir things up and not you? Why do I dig up
my family's stories and you let yours
be buried? Afraid of what you might find out?"
What would German children find
if they reached into the back of the family's cupboards,
poked about in the deep drawers?
An old box?
Old photos old uniforms old beliefs old
murders
their family did not
prevent.
I wash my hands, dry them on my jeans.
We walk out of the washroom.
I relent
"You got your hand slapped once, eh."

She nods.

"Been there" I bridge.

QUESTIONNAIRE
GRANDCHILDREN AND GREAT-GRANDCHILDREN
OF SURVIVORS

How wide the scars
How present the danger
How knowing the cells
How far the continuing reach   ?

POSTCARD TO THE HOLOCAUST

dear daughter ziva,

     what comfort is a parent who is afraid of monsters
after you woke from your first frightening dream   I tried to say
my lines   *There is nothing to be afraid of Everything is all right*
Mommy and Daddy are here We won't let anyone

     my fear clamped down   the best I could offer was
I've got you We're okay You're in my arms You're as safe as
I can make you

     each night while we nurse hugged in the rocking chair
I sing our own lullaby borrowing the tune of Amazing Grace
Bless this day for we have gained   given much   and lost nothing
Blessed was yesterday for we did gain   give much   and lose nothing
Blessed be tomorrow that we may gain   give much   and lose nothing

     it surprised me the first time you suddenly sang along
how much you had learned just from listening the sound of the words
the tune bang on and so so sweet

     now I overhear you singing our lullaby as you nurse your
bears and dolls resting them across your lap and tucking them close
around you   the meaning of the words unfolding the comfort you
can give   that must be the comfort I have given you   voice: attentive
clear ready   a bright thing to hold up and out to the lurking world
a talisman

Dr. jur. *Joseph D. Borgida*
Notary Public

TELEPHONE: 925-5611
EVENINGS: HU. 1-2607

455 SPADINA AVE., SUITE 201
TORONTO 179. ONTARIO

August 4th, 1972

Mr. Roman Mandel.
Toronto 12, Ont.

Dear Mr. Mandel:

I am pleased to advise you that I received the decision of the restitution office concerning your claim, and this decision is favorable for you.

You were granted

in a lump sum (Kapitalentschaedigung)	DM 6.438.-
in accumulated pensions until August 31st, 1972	" 31.525.-
total	DM 37.963.-

From September 1st, 1972 you'll receive a monthly pension in the amount of DM 2o9.-

You were granted the compensation because of

"chronic affective disturbances "

on the basis of a disability of 3o%.

With this decision we must be pleased and therefore I do not intend to lodge an appeal against it. I hope that you share my opinion.

In order to have the money paid in Germany, we have to prove that you are alive. For this purpose please be here

on Friday, August 11th, 1972 at 9.3o A.M.

bringing along a certificate of identity with your photograph. A valid passport or the miniature Certificate of Canadian Citizenship are adequate proofs.

Should you be unable to be here at the date and hour given above, please call us on the phone and we will agree on another date.

I am pleased indeed that our efforts led to full success and remain

yours very truly

Dr. jur. JOSEPH D. BORGIDA
Richter beim Rumaenischen
Tafelgericht in Cluj und Bochtas   *f. Joseph Borgida -*
OEFFENTLICHER NOTAR
(NOTARY PUBLIC)
455 Spadina Ave. - Toronto 4, Ont.

Mr. Brown

Letter notifying Roman Mandel he has been granted reparations payments
by the German Indemnification Office, 1972

HOW TO TELL YOUR CHILDREN ABOUT THE HOLOCAUST

I.

Damage Control

Dad,
you treat the subject: *'Holocaust'*
like something that slipped out against your will,
an abuse you tried to avoid.

'Child of Survivors'
something done to you
by your parents
that you would not do
to your children.
'Survivor'
a label foisted on you
to explain.
Explain what?
You balk.

But you are foiled by those
not as adept as you
at keeping memories to themselves.
Foiled by illogic, the inexplicable,
by transcendence, blood ties and ESP,
by irrepressible osmosis
no feat of logic,
no skilful minimizing
can inhibit or tame.

Personal history arrives
of its own volition,
no consent
no map
no help
no tricks.
You are merely here
to explain it.

II.

Be Happy

"Dead . . . dead . . . all dead.
My family . . . your relatives. Dead.
Murdered.
Now go . . . be happy."

III.

Tell Your Children

Tell them nothing.
Tell them everything.
Over and over again.
Imply it in everything you say.
>   *Keep it a secret. A dark one.*

Tell them when they ask.
When they are ready.
When you are ready.
When they least expect it!
>   *Before bed. Nighty night!*

Remind them each time they complain.
Mean well.
Leave out the worst.
When they are thirteen.
>   *One at a time.*
>   *Calmly.*

Tell them when they catch you crying in the hall.
When they ask about your screaming nightmares.
When they go into therapy.
>   *When they drag the family*
>   *into it.*

Tell them when you realize they figured it out.
Muster all your strength.
Practice with strangers.
Start small.
    Stick to the highlights.

Tell them when the family is together.
When you bee-line away from a TV special on the Nazi SS.
On your death bed.
When there is nothing else to tell.
    Make them beg. *You must be certain.*

Tell them before it's too late.
Not *too* early.
If it comes up in their schooling.
When they have children of their own.
    After your life-threatening heart attack.

Tell them when you suspect it has affected them.
Regardless of your intentions.
When they notice you *always* expect the worst.
And so do they.
    When it is misrepresented.
    When it is denied.

Tell them after your first related conference.
When they see your reparations cheque from the German government.
Let them figure it out.
    Just tell them. No big deal.

Tell them when they seem too comfy.
When you discover they need to know.
Only if they won't get all upset.
 When somebody else lets it out of the bag.

Timing is crucial.
You'll never get it right.
Beware of guilt.
 When you admit that secrets are parasitic.
 And hearty as insects.

Co-ordinate the event with your spouse.
Prepare yourself for the worst.
Establish ground rules.
When you can contain the emotional fallout.
 When you don't have plans for the next day.

Tell   your   children.

Whenever.   However.   For whatever reason.

Before you are the last Holocaust Survivor on earth.

Promise me.

IV.

Why

Your silence
draws treacherous lines
between what harms
hinders
protects
sustains
heals   us

dear mom,

      both   you were right and wrong I didn't know
what I was getting into   neither did you neither did any
of us   our scattered past collected weighed and no
harm came didn't destroy dad nor anyone else

      victory shared   this book you hold   our efforts
what we anticipate what we get what we wish   wrestling
tending mending gathering blending daily becoming
something other than we were   our lives stunningly parallel
simultaneous redolent of each other   you and I   devoted
herders   our vulnerable non-complacent flocks

Amt für Wiedergutmachung in Saarburg
Heckingstraße 31 · 54439 **Saarburg**
Postfach 1465   54434 Saarburg
SB/RA-Nr. 23/061635 2

1994

Lebensbescheinigung
Certificate of Life

Falls Ihre Anschrift sich geändert hat, geben Sie
bitte nachstehend Ihre neue Anschrift an.
If you have changed your address, please enter
the new one below.

Herrn/Frau
ROMAN MANDEL

TORONTO ONT
KANADA

Official Certificate   **Amtliche Bescheinigung**   Erläuterungen s. Rückseite
(for indemnification   (nur für Zwecke der Wiedergut-   Explanatory Notes please turn over
purposes only)   machung)

Es wird bescheinigt, daß die nachstehend genannte rentenberechtigte Person
This is to certify that the undernamed person entitled to a pension

MANDEL   ROMAN   (Raymond)   geboren am 15/7/1935
(Familienname, bei Frauen auch Geburtsname, Vorname)   born on
(family name – women also maiden name – first name)

wohnhaft in _____ TORONTO, ONTARIO, CANADA M4R 1K6
residing at

am Leben ist.   Familienstand married
is still alive.   marital status

Sie ist **persönlich vor mir erschienen** und hat ihre Identität nachgewiesen durch
He/She **personaly appeared before me** and has proved his/her identity by means of

PASSEPORT   Nr. MB 895675
(Art des Ausweises)   No.
(nature of identity document)

                    US-residents: Social-Security-Number please: _____
Die nachstehende Unterschrift ist von ihr selbst geleistet worden:
He/She has written the following signature himself/herself:

(Unterschrift der rentenberechtigten Person)
(signature of person entitled to a pension)

                                      Toronto, Canada den AUG 22, 94
R Mandel   (Ort)
                                      (place and date)

(Unterschrift und Amtsbezeichnung der bescheinigenden Person)
(signature and official designation of person issuing the certificate)

'94

(Bezeichnung und Dienstsiegel der bescheinigenden Stelle)
(designation and official stamp of issuing authority)

(Raum für Legalisation)

Certificate of Life, signed annually in the presence of the German consul, 1994

TOGETHER

"What was there to tell?" was my father's response
when pressed all these years later for information.
Both of us defensive. I wanted it
retroactively. Calling him on a debt, finally, as if
a father owes his child the story of his life,

all of it, no matter the cost of telling, no matter
the reasons for having not told. My birthright.
Out with it, sit down like a spider
on a good day - the perfect array of breeze,
branches and leaves, the absence

of invasive passersby - and spin
a complete, precise web in which to settle,
to live out the rest of life. I wanted to know and to know,
to span the before, the after, the skin, bone, guts
of our family history. The long-anticipated moment

of truth. As if a child can prepare for the onslaught
of a parent's life. Comfortable chairs, hot
tea, milk, one piece of dark chocolate each
to melt too quickly inside the cheek with every sip.   Actually,
it wasn't like that at all. It was over the phone

with faceless safety and no need
to avert our eyes. I just grabbed the receiver,
possessed by a tiny fact banging unbearably
about my skull without sense or context.
Made brave by my obsessive craving

to piece things together. A deceptively modest desire.
The odds mercilessly against us. For me, and worse,
for my father, the longing could never be met
by what little he remembered. For he had been a child then,
and later, no one thought it necessary

to keep his years in Poland sharp in his mind.
Those times were talked about little, if at all.
A past kept at low volume, held cautiously
at bay. His memory wasn't tended like a trust
that would accumulate, prove invaluable in the years to come.

This, too, passed to me, this lack of training,
practising memory. Unlike my friends, I remember
little of childhood. My parents were not in the habit
of recounting anecdotes. Perhaps my mother
took her cue from my father, not wanting to fling him

back in time, not wanting to retain in her life what had been cut
from his. Without their example, I didn't learn
to collect my childhood experiences.
Clothespin them securely to a steady line.
Fold them away in a basket or drawer for easy reach.

Even I could not narrate my life the way I asked of my father.
It is more like a web sliced through by storm and wind and arms.
Yet, I wanted to catch
what I had been missing, what I needed.
Maybe, it had dawned on him, he missed and needed, too.

The telling. Was it not his birthright. The silence,
unfair. On the phone, his voice lifetimes away,
he curiously observed our measured sparring,
a far off shadow play. Bemused, holding his life
between his thumb and index finger, close

to his eyes, seeing it anew and squinting to discover
what drew my attention. He was intimidated and
intrigued by my interest. I had to prove myself,
"Father, I have caught this burning ball. And will not
carry it alone." And he began, "It's like

anything else. I remember. And I don't remember."
Small questions and small answers. I realized
as I listened to him, much of this I already know.
Somehow. I must have been told
more than I thought. And thought, more than I was told.

We talk in periodic spurts, with trepidation,
it is never comfortable or easy. Haltingly
over time, separately and together, piecing
small answers and small questions.
Each word a reclamation.

Ray (Roman) Mandel, New Jewish Cemetery, Cracow, 1996

POSTCARD TO THE HOLOCAUST

dear dad,

you and my daughter Ziva rig a trapeze from your high basement ceiling run away to the circus   you coax her from one acrobatic challenge to the next   she your enraptured autonomous puppet   you her gleeful ring leader

it is true parents are reborn with their children and their grandchildren   visibly invisibly we shift roles follow lead trade   I went to Poland came back alive then you and mom followed   exactly three years later retracing our steps   we picked you up at the airport with Ziva returning the favour sharing badges of courage   Ziva pulled you outside   you exclaimed disbelieving   *Cracow, it was like I had been away one minute!* *One minute.*

Ruth Mandel in 1993 and Ray Mandel in 1996, New Jewish Cemetery, Cracow

GHOST STORIES

These partial stories, forgotten stories, gaps
in stories, detailed stories, these unfinished
stories, over and done with stories, stories
hidden in stories, stories hidden by stories,
these shards of stories, hints of stories, dead-
end stories, these spiralling stories, stories with
unknown endings, tellable stories, unmentionable
stories, repressed stories, these highlights-only
stories, oft-repeated stories, filtered stories,
fleeting-snippet childhood stories, these before
stories, after stories, trailing-off stories, these
spiked stories, like-yesterday stories
haunt us

and they will,
until we have them all, all,
exactly. And then,
mortal, they will haunt us
still.

A FAMILY TREE BY NUMBERS

If the concentration camps had been liberated in 1943 or 1944
I could have done my family tree
by numbers.
Now only one such branch, Auschwitz-Birkenau 6 4 1 8 9,
(my great aunt Erna)
still smoulders from the brand
against unwilling skin.

My uncle Henryk is the child
neighbours promised to protect.
They threw him onto the street,
denounced him at the age of nine,
they kicked him and kicked him.
And I am told that my grandmother
knew in a dream from her hiding place
that he was made to bleed to death slowly
on the street.

My grandmother Henia finds her grave
softer now
on the branch that is my middle name.
And same too
my great grandmother Ruth
about whom I can know almost nothing.

My father Roman (Raymond now),
a small child then,
receives *reparations payments* from the German government.
In spite of his fear, he has grafted

three children to absent bark.
In spite of the flames stalking him,
searing his offspring,
transferring the genetically coded
Warning

that who I am
must never be decided
by uninvited courts

Warning
That who I am
must never be selected *(that word)*
not for one split second
not ever
not on my life

That if ever I am only a Jew to a Nazi
only a woman to a man
only a soldier to an army
only an obstacle to a bullet

If ever I am only
a number or a name

Then surely
     I am
     on fire
     again.

TERMS

Belzec was a death camp in eastern Poland.

The *bimah* is the elevated platform from which the service is conducted in many synagogues.

Cosmos are prolific, self-seeding flowers.

Displaced Persons were those who survived the war and, for a variety of reasons, could not return to their homes.

Little stones refer to the Jewish custom of leaving stones on a grave to mark a visit.

A *mezuzah* is a small, decorative container that can be affixed to the door frames in a Jewish home, and contains a small parchment scroll of words of one's own choosing or a traditional blessing.

Polaks, meaning Polish people, is an idiom from the 'old-country', which is the speaker's cultural context, and is not used here as contemporary slang.

Reparations payments refers here to a highly restrictive compensation program called Wiedergutmachung, meaning "making good again," which was established by the post-war West German government in response to organized pressure from Holocaust survivors. Claimants had to prove they suffered continued hardship as a direct result of wartime Nazi persecution. The program administrators assigned a rating to the hardship, as a basis on which to accord compensation. Those in receipt of reparations payments must present themselves annually to the German consul to prove they are alive.

Shabbat marks the seventh day of the week as a day of rest and reflection, beginning Friday evening with a dinner and blessings of one's choosing over candles, wine and braided challah.

Shoah is the Hebrew word for the Holocaust.

Volksdeutch was the Nazi designation for a Polish citizen with some German family lineage.

Zaidi is the Yiddish word for grandfather.

LIST OF ILLUSTRATIONS

ACKNOWLEDGMENTS

Twelve years is a lot of folks to keep track of – a long quilting bee. I must first thank my families – the family I was born into and the family I have created – in that peculiar way that one thanks family, after all the trials and tribulations (and up-sides too). Thanks Dad for the childhood memories and your slant on historical events in Poland and Eastern Europe during the war. That said, all sentiments and assertions are my own.

As the saying goes 'It takes a village to raise a child' and so too to write a book. For motivating me with peer support and a sense of audience, I wish to thank the folks who have published or presented my poetry in their books, anthologies, journals, newsletters, websites and readings, many of which are listed up front. And the Ontario Arts Council for the Writers' Reserve Grant awarded to me by Women's Press in 1994, the Canada Council for the Explorations Grant awarded to me in 1995, and the Toronto Arts Council's Grant to Writers awarded to me in 1995. And the many instructors and participants who have mentored me at various poetry workshops: Don McKay at Sage Hill, Marge Piercy at Elat Chayim, Suniti Namjoshi at West Word IX, Rhea Tregebov at Ryerson University. My gratitude to these workshops is multiplied by the friends I made. At Elat Chayim, I met Ann Decter, who became my steady editor and now, determined publisher. At Sage Hill I met Jannie Edwards, who has helped me edit each poem into this book.

I give my most gracious thanks (in non-hierarchical order, sort of first letter alphabetically) to the individuals and groups who have made it possible for me to tread, sink and swim: Ann Decter; Barbara Walther (high school English teacher); my utterly-loved children and dogs and their adoring care-givers; my ever-there Ian Clifford; good buddies; Jacquie Buncel; Jannie Edwards; justice and anti-discrimination educators, activists and artists whose work is heartening and saves lives; Laurie Pine; Lindsey Tashlin; the various professionals who keep my life in running order; Elzbieta Lembas and the Righteous Polish families whom we visited in Poland and whose model I wish to honour and follow; Robert Jan van Pelt; Sharon Weintraub; Shoah Survivors and their children like and unlike me; Sir Martin Gilbert; Zelda Abramson; our companions while in Poland Sophie Read, Sonia Lucas and Beata Lakomiec; anyone to whom I know I am grateful yet whose name I have missed; and to my favourite poems and novels and their writers, whose words I needed, to bring forth my own.